Enough With the Insanity

Restore the Republic

R. L. Womac

authorHOUSE®

AuthorHouse™
1663 Liberty Drive
Bloomington, IN 47403
www.authorhouse.com
Phone: 1-800-839-8640

First published by AuthorHouse   6/25/2010

ISBN: 978-1-4520-2733-3 (e)
ISBN: 978-1-4520-2732-6 (sc)
ISBN: 978-1-4520-2731-9 (hc)

Library of Congress Control Number: 2010907649

Printed in the United States of America
Bloomington, Indiana

This book is printed on acid-free paper.

Introduction

I hate to admit at the completion of this book I have been unemployed for over a year. Never in my 44 years of living have I ever been unemployed for this amount of time. In the time period of the last year I have lost my home, seen plenty of other people do the same and have began to lose hope. I was luckier than some; I had the old house I grew up in to move into. I didn't want that, I wanted to keep the home I had been paying on and had just lost, the old house was falling in and all the family had stuff stored there. This place was packed thru with old clothes, toys, furniture, doll collections, and junk was the way I looked at it. The floor was rotten in places, the walls warped, and dusty and dirty it definitely was. So with some help from family and friends I moved my possessions into this old drafty and dirty house I had escaped from years ago.

I asked my mom why did she have so much junk in there, old

clothes, pictures, toys, and such. Well that didn't go well, she broke down and went to crying and told me do whatever I wanted with the contents, she didn't have a storage building to put the stuff in, so do what I wanted with it. I told her that I would go through it and what was important I would keep for her and the junk I would get rid of. Well that backfired in a good way on me I guess. As I was cleaning out a spot to begin living in I started finding things that brought memories back of growing up. Pictures, toys, clothes, books, moms whatnots, and even the old bowl that she always made gravy in. That's when the trouble began. That's when I had to give in and admit that this was not junk. So I called Mom and told her I was wrong, it was not junk it was her and our lives and our family's history and I would be very careful on what I got rid of. So as I kept digging into this eclectic collection of stuff I found one of my old treasures she had kept. A bunch of old history books and a collection of the writings of Thomas Jefferson. Well I had to take a break, you know what I mean?

I took to reading at night before going to sleep; I found our country's history about as fascinating and eclectic as my own family's. I was looking at these books and listening to the news and I heard how our government was going to bail out these businesses and banks and how they are going to take control of them and I thought whoa, wait a minute. This sounds awful familiar. Then they want to raise all these taxes on savings, IRA's and bonuses, it sounded very familiar. So I reread some of the chapters I had just read in the old history books I had and I knew why it sounded so familiar, this attitude was why this country came into existence. We formed this country and revolted on Great Britain for some of the very same things. No President or Congress or Senate of the United States of America has that kind of power. Nor that kind of authority for that matter, but I'm getting ahead of myself.

And that is when I decided to write this book. Our country has become like my old house in being rundown and falling in. We have all kinds of infestations; lobbyists, special interest groups, senators and congressmen not doing the will of the people, and a president acting like a king. In the following chapters you the reader will find the legitimate bounds of the President, senate, congress and some ideas on how to deal with the problems this country is facing. Please read on carefully and attentively.

Chapter One
Introduction to our Type of Government

We the People of the United States, in Order to form a more perfect Union, establish Justice, insure domestic Tranquility, provide for the common defence, promote the general Welfare, and secure the Blessings of Liberty to ourselves and our Posterity, do ordain and establish this Constitution for the United States of America.

The above is the preamble to the Constitution of the United States of America. If you are under 40 years old you probably have never heard of it. When I was in school we were required to memorize this important piece of our history. Now as you read on you will be given quotes from the man who wrote the Declaration of Independence, Thomas Jefferson. A former President and one of the architects of our country and form of government, which qualifies him as knowing how they wanted our system to work, don't you think?

Now lets set some things straight right off the bat, form of government, Republican. That's right, Republican not democracy. Our teachers and government on one of our most basic things have misled a lot of people.

There are some misconceptions that a lot of people have about our country. The biggest is that we are the greatest democracy in the world. We were not founded as a democracy at all. This country was founded as a republic: remember the pledge of allegiance? " And to the republic for which it stands", is the quote. What you are going to read next is from the Constitution of The United States.

Article IV - The States　　Section 4 - Republican government

The United States shall guarantee to every State in this Union a ***Republican*** Form of Government, and shall protect each of them against Invasion; and on Application of the Legislature, or of the Executive (when the Legislature cannot be convened) against domestic Violence.

Get you a copy of the Constitution and look for yourself.

What's the difference you ask? You tell me after you read what's next. The following are quotes from Thomas Jefferson. Since he was there when this country was founded I'm sure he knew what they meant when they formed this country's system of government.

"From the moment that to preserve our rights a change of government became necessary, no doubt could be entertained that a republican form was most consonant with reason, with right, with the freedom of man, and with the character and situation of our fellow citizens." --Thomas Jefferson: Reply to Virginia Legislature, 1809. ME 16:333

"The people through all the States are for republican forms, republican principles, simplicity, economy, religious and civil freedom." --Thomas Jefferson to Edward Livingston, 1800. ME 10:164

"[Our] object is to secure self-government by the republicanism of our constitution, as well as by the spirit of the people; and to nourish and perpetuate that spirit. I am not among those who fear the people. They and not the rich are our dependence for continued freedom." --Thomas Jefferson to Samuel Kercheval, 1816. ME 15:39

The difference between a republic and a democracy can be brought out simply. Rome was a democracy with senators and an emperor. The senate could vote on things but the emperor could still basically do, as he wanted. The senators could eventually be replaced. They listened to the people and voted to present laws to the emperor. The people had representatives that really didn't answer to them. You also in a democracy have what can basically be called, mob rule. The bigger groups get what they want regardless of people's rights.

In a republic you have elected representatives too. Your elected representatives answer to the people. You the citizens are the supreme power in a republic because you are telling your elected representatives what to do and what kind of laws you want. They are to work for you in your place at the seat of government. Read the following quotes; let me remind you once again that this man wrote the Declaration of Independence. He knew what kind of government they were creating.

"A government is republican in proportion as every member composing it has his equal voice in the direction of its concerns: not indeed in person, which would be impracticable beyond the limits of a city or small township, but <u>by representatives chosen by himself and responsible to him at short periods.</u>" --Thomas Jefferson to Samuel Kercheval, 1816. ME 15:33

"Action by the citizens in person, in affairs within their reach and competence, and in all others by representatives, <u>chosen immediately, and removable by themselves,</u> constitutes the essence of a republic... All governments are more or less republican in proportion as this principle enters more or less into their composition." --Thomas Jefferson to Pierre Samuel Dupont de Nemours, 1816. ME 14:490

"[To establish republican government, it is necessary to] effect a constitution in which the will of the nation shall have an organized control over the actions of its government, and its citizens a regular

protection against its oppressions."
--Thomas Jefferson to Lafayette, 1816.
ME 19:240

"We think experience has proved it safer for the mass of individuals composing the society to reserve to themselves personally the exercise of all rightful powers to which they are competent and to delegate those to which they are not competent to <u>deputies named and removable for unfaithful conduct by themselves immediately</u>." --Thomas Jefferson to Pierre Samuel Dupont de Nemours, 1816. ME 14:487

"The whole body of the nation is the sovereign legislative, judiciary, and executive power for itself. The inconvenience of meeting to exercise these powers in person, and their inaptitude to exercise them, induce them to appoint special organs to declare their legislative will, to judge and to execute it. <u>It is the will of the nation which makes the law obligatory; it is their will which creates or annihilates the organ which is to declare and announce it.</u> They may do it by a single person, as an emperor of Russia (constituting his declarations evidence of their will), or by a few persons, as the aristocracy of Venice, or by a complication of councils, as in our former regal government or our present republican one. The law being law because it is the will of the nation, is not changed by their changing the organ through which they choose to announce their future will; no more than the acts I have done by one attorney lose their obligation by my changing or discontinuing that attorney." --Thomas Jefferson to Edmund Randolph, 1799. ME 10:126

I do believe with confidence I have shown you the reader that our government was not formed as a Democracy. To some it may have come as a shock but we must now press on to the next chapter. Now can you tell the difference between a republic and mob rule democracy? In a republic the people and not their elected representatives are the supreme power. Self government is what we wanted and got originally, my question to you the reader is this; what happened to make this country the way it is now?

Chapter Two
The Bill of Rights

If the shock of chapter one was bad wait till you read this chapter. The words in this chapter would send most senators and congressmen into a fit.

You the American citizen have rights not touchable by Congress or the Senate or even the President. You the citizen have rights that are guaranteed and were heavily fought for. Look at the next set of quotes.

"If we are made in some degree for others, yet in a greater are we made for ourselves. It were contrary to feeling and indeed ridiculous to suppose that a man had less rights in himself than one of his neighbors, or all of them put together. <u>This would be slavery, and not that liberty which the bill of rights has made inviolable, and for the preservation of which our government has been charged.</u>" --Thomas Jefferson to James Monroe, 1782. ME 4:196, Papers 6:185

"A bill of rights is what the people are entitled to against every government on earth, general or particular; and what no just government should refuse, or rest on inferences." --Thomas Jefferson to James Madison, 1787. ME 6:388, Papers 12:440

"The general voice from north to south... calls for a bill of rights. It seems pretty generally understood that this should go to juries, habeas corpus, standing armies, printing, religion and monopolies. I conceive there may be difficulty in finding general modifications of these suited to the habits of all the States. But if such cannot be found, then it is better to establish trials by jury, the right of habeas corpus, freedom of the press, and freedom of religion, in all cases, and to abolish standing armies in time of peace, and monopolies in all cases, than not to do it in any. The few cases wherein these things may do evil cannot be weighed against the multitude wherein the want of them will do evil." --Thomas Jefferson to James Madison, 1788. ME 7:96

"*I hope, therefore, a bill of rights will be formed to guard the people against the federal government as they are already guarded against their State governments, in most instances.*" --Thomas Jefferson to James Madison, 1788. ME 7:98

"[The first step is] to concur in a declaration of rights, at least, so that the nation may be acknowledged to have some fundamental rights not alterable by their ordinary legislature, and that this may form a ground work for future improvements." --Thomas Jefferson to John Jay, 1788.

Now I know that there are a lot of quotes here but it is for a good reason. You hear all these politicians stating they are acting as the Founding Fathers would, baloney. Today Thomas Jefferson and the others would be branded as domestic terrorists and thrown in Gitmo. Look at the dates on the quotes and look

11

at the time frame. Your Bill of rights was fought for heavily and argued about for a while.

The above quote shows what they wanted in a government. Rights that cannot be changed or messed with at all. You are guaranteed these rights, every American citizen.

As you noticed there was a lot of work put into giving every American citizen the Bill of Rights. Now I want you the reader to read them for yourself.

Here are your unchangeable rights.

Amendment 1 - Freedom of Religion, Press, Expression. Ratified 12/15/1791

Congress shall make no law respecting an establishment of religion, or prohibiting the free exercise thereof; or abridging the freedom of speech, or of the press; or the right of the people peaceably to assemble, and to petition the Government for a redress of grievances.

Amendment 2 - Right to Bear Arms. Ratified 12/15/1791.

A well regulated Militia, being necessary to the security of a free State, the right of the people to keep and bear Arms, shall not be infringed.

Amendment 3 - Quartering of Soldiers. Ratified 12/15/1791

No Soldier shall, in time of peace be quartered in any house, without the consent of the Owner, nor in time of war, but in a manner to be prescribed by law.

Amendment 4 - Search and Seizure. Ratified 12/15/1791.

The right of the people to be secure in their persons, houses, papers, and effects, against unreasonable searches and seizures, shall not be violated, and no Warrants shall issue, but upon probable cause, supported by Oath or affirmation, and particularly describing the place to be searched, and the persons or things to be seized.

Amendment 5 - Trial and Punishment, Compensation for Takings. Ratified 12/15/1791.

No person shall be held to answer for a capital, or otherwise infamous crime, unless on a presentment or indictment of a Grand Jury, except in cases arising in the land or naval forces, or in the Militia, when in actual service in time of

War or public danger; nor shall any person be subject for the same offense to be twice put in jeopardy of life or limb; nor shall be compelled in any criminal case to be a witness against himself, nor be deprived of life, liberty, or property, without due process of law; nor shall private property be taken for public use, without just compensation.

Amendment 6 - Right to Speedy Trial, Confrontation of Witnesses. Ratified 12/15/1791.

In all criminal prosecutions, the accused shall enjoy the right to a speedy and public trial, by an impartial jury of the State and district wherein the crime shall have been committed, which district shall have been previously ascertained by law, and to be informed of the nature and cause of the accusation; to be confronted with the witnesses against him; to have compulsory process for obtaining witnesses in his favor, and to have the Assistance of Counsel for his defence.

Amendment 7 - Trial by Jury in Civil Cases. Ratified 12/15/1791.

In Suits at common law, where the value in controversy shall exceed twenty dollars, the right of trial by jury shall be preserved, and no fact tried by a jury, shall be otherwise reexamined in any Court of the United States, than according to the rules of the common law.

Amendment 8 - Cruel and Unusual Punishment. Ratified 12/15/1791.

Excessive bail shall not be required, nor excessive fines imposed, nor cruel and unusual punishments inflicted.

Amendment 9 - Construction of Constitution. Ratified 12/15/1791.

The enumeration in the Constitution, of certain rights, shall not be construed to deny or disparage others retained by the people.

Amendment 10 - Powers of the States and People. Ratified 12/15/1791. The powers not delegated to the United States by the Constitution, nor prohibited by it to the States, are reserved to the States respectively, or to the people.

Now I don't know about you but to me these are pretty self-explanatory. Doesn't it seem that our elected officials need a little refresher course where these are concerned?

Now after reading all of this are you sure our government today is the same one described in the quotes you read? I want you the reader to see in the words of one of the Founders of this country what they intended when they formed the country. An American citizen has a unique birthright that no other person has ever had. The country and government were to work hand in hand. You were to be a free man or woman with rights given that no other country had ever given its people.

The American people have 2 choices.

1. Do nothing and let things continue as they are.

2. Make them stop and change this country back to the way it was. The new American Revolution will be to reclaim what was lost, not for something new.

How many of the rights that were given in the Constitution are being chipped away at or being thrown out the window by the people in Washington today? Now I dare say that the only people to blame for this being done are the American people themselves. How dare you say that, you might ask. I say it because of this.

"The spirit of the times may alter, will alter. Our rulers will become corrupt, our people careless. A single zealot may commence persecutor, and better men be his victims. It can never be too often repeated that the time for fixing every essential right on a legal basis is while our rulers are honest and ourselves united. From the conclusion of [their] war [for independence, a nation begins] going down hill. It will not then be necessary to resort every moment to the people for support. They will be forgotten, therefore, and their rights disregarded. They will forget themselves but in the sole faculty of making money, and will never think of uniting to effect a due respect for their rights. The shackles, therefore, which shall not be knocked off at the conclusion of [that] war will remain on [them] long, will be made heavier and heavier, till [their] rights

shall revive or expire in a convulsion."
--Thomas Jefferson: Notes on Virginia
Q.XVII, 1782. (*) ME 2:225

"To secure these [inalienable] rights [to life, liberty, and the pursuit of happiness], governments are instituted among men, deriving their just powers from the consent of the governed... Whenever any form of government becomes destructive of these ends, it is the right of the people to alter or abolish it, and to institute new government, laying its foundation on such principles, and organizing its powers in such form, as to them shall seem most likely to effect their safety and happiness." - Thomas Jefferson: Declaration of Independence, 1776. ME 1:29, Papers 1:429

All I have to say is this, these are your rights and it's up to you to use them. What we have in government now is doing everything it can to deny you the rights you were given. It is time to stop the insanity that is going on in the halls of power in this country!

Do you see the point I am trying to make?

Chapter Three
Congress and The Senate Responsibilities

Now in this chapter I want to show you the reader what senators and congressmen are to do. The following is straight out of the Constitution of the United States of America. This Constitution defines what powers and limitations these United States; literally uniting states agreed to give senators, members of congress and the president. They telling their elected representative what they would allow did this. The following as I already stated is directly taken from the Constitution of The United States.

Article I - The Legislative Branch Section 8 - Powers of Congress

The Congress shall have Power To lay and collect Taxes, Duties, Imposts and Excises, to pay the Debts and provide for the common Defence and general Welfare of the United States; but all Duties, Imposts and Excises shall be uniform throughout the United States;

To borrow money on the credit of the United States;

To regulate Commerce with foreign Nations, and among the several States, and with the Indian Tribes;

To establish an uniform Rule of Naturalization, and uniform Laws on the subject of Bankruptcies throughout the United States;

To coin Money, regulate the Value thereof, and of foreign Coin, and fix the Standard of Weights and Measures;

To provide for the Punishment of counterfeiting the Securities and current Coin of the United States;

To establish Post Offices and Post Roads;

To promote the Progress of Science and useful Arts, by securing for limited Times to Authors and Inventors the exclusive Right to their respective Writings and Discoveries;

To constitute Tribunals inferior to the supreme Court;

To define and punish Piracies and Felonies committed on the high Seas, and Offenses against the Law of Nations;

To declare War, grant Letters of Marque and Reprisal, and make Rules concerning Captures on Land and Water;

To raise and support Armies, but no Appropriation of Money to that Use shall be for a longer Term than two Years;

To provide and maintain a Navy;

To make Rules for the Government and Regulation of the land and naval Forces;

To provide for calling forth the Militia to execute the Laws of the Union, suppress Insurrections and repel Invasions;

To provide for organizing, arming, and disciplining the Militia, and for governing such Part of them as may be employed in the Service of the United States, reserving to the States respectively, the Appointment of the Officers, and the Authority of training the Militia according to the discipline prescribed by Congress;

To exercise exclusive Legislation in all Cases whatsoever, over such District (not exceeding ten Miles square) as may, by Cession of particular States, and the acceptance of Congress, become the Seat of the Government of the United States, and to exercise like Authority over all Places purchased by the Consent of the Legislature of the State in which the Same shall be, for the Erection of Forts, Magazines, Arsenals, dock-Yards, and other needful Buildings; And

To make all Laws which shall be necessary and proper for carrying into Execution the foregoing Powers, and all other

Powers vested by this Constitution in the Government of the United States, or in any Department or Officer thereof.

Now I want you to look above at this, (The Congress shall have Power To lay and collect

Taxes, Duties, Imposts and Excises, to pay the Debts and provide for the common Defence and general Welfare of the United States; but all Duties, Imposts and Excises shall be uniform throughout the United States;)

Read the next quotes carefully.

"[We] disavow and declare to be most false and unfounded, the doctrine that the compact, in authorizing its federal branch to lay and collect taxes, duties, imposts and excises to pay the debts and provide for the common defence and general welfare of the United States, has given them thereby a power to do whatever they may think or pretend would promote the general welfare, which construction would make that, of itself, a complete government, without limitation of powers; but that the plain sense and obvious meaning were, that they might levy the taxes necessary to provide for the general welfare by the various acts of power therein specified and delegated to them, and by no others." --Thomas Jefferson: Declaration and Protest of Virginia, 1825. ME 17:444

"Unless the mass retains sufficient control over those entrusted with the powers of their government, these will be perverted to their own oppression, and to the perpetuation of wealth and power in the individuals and their families selected for the trust." --Thomas Jefferson to M. van der Kemp, 1812. ME 13:136

Now I don't know about you but the above quotes are very easily understood. When you take into consideration the form of government we have in a republic. The Constitution spells out what they can do and what they cannot. We the people of the country are their bosses not the other way around. Read what Dr. Franklin had to say about who was in charge.

Benjamin Franklin wrote, *"In free governments the*

rulers are the servants and the people their superiors and sovereigns."

You now have in office a senate, congress, and a president going against the will of the people in blatant arrogance. This healthcare bill is not wanted. The people have an out of control government that does not answer to them or dare I say anyone. Let me show you their limitations according to what is supposed to be our Constitution.

Section 9 - Limits on Congress

The Migration or Importation of such Persons as any of the States now existing shall think proper to admit, shall not be prohibited by the Congress prior to the Year one thousand eight hundred and eight, but a tax or duty may be imposed on such Importation, not exceeding ten dollars for each Person.

The privilege of the Writ of Habeas Corpus shall not be suspended, unless when in Cases of Rebellion or Invasion the public Safety may require it.

No Bill of Attainder or ex post facto Law shall be passed.

(No capitation, or other direct, Tax shall be laid, unless in

Proportion to the Census or Enumeration herein before directed to be taken.) **(Section in parentheses clarified by the 16th Amendment.)**

No Tax or Duty shall be laid on Articles exported from any State.

No Preference shall be given by any Regulation of Commerce or Revenue to the Ports of one State over those of another: nor shall Vessels bound to, or from, one State, be obliged to enter, clear, or pay Duties in another.

No Money shall be drawn from the Treasury, but in Consequence of Appropriations made by Law; and a regular Statement and Account of the Receipts and Expenditures of all public Money shall be published from time to time.

No Title of Nobility shall be granted by the United States: And no Person holding any Office of Profit or Trust under them, shall, without the Consent of the Congress, accept of any present, Emolument, Office, or Title, of any kind whatever, from any King, Prince or foreign State.

Notice the title of nobility phrase above. Now I will give them credit that they have not declared themselves nobility but they are beginning to act like they are. The congress and senate getting their raises and more money by taking it from the people. Acting like royalty instead of public servants, passing laws that they don't keep themselves. Do you remember the

Congressional post office fiasco years ago? What about all the senators and congressmen not paying their taxes. What about the guys Obama nominated for positions that didn't pay their taxes. I know we would have lost everything we had and probably went to prison if that had been you the reader or myself.

I also want you the reader to notice the arrogance and preening that they do when in public. This president spent more of your tax dollars on parties than anyone on record. This present speaker of the house proclaiming she doesn't answer to the people who elected her; telling the American people they don't need to know what is in the health bill. What the American people need to know is this; you have the right to put each of them out of office now! You don't have to wait till the election. They are overstepping their bounds constitutionally and legally. We have a group of Senators and Congressmen and dare I say a President now who is going crazy on taking our liberty and freedom away as quick as possible. I would say that something is terribly wrong in this country now wouldn't you? Now I want to bring to your attention something else. It seems most of our leaders today all lack two things. Most of them are lawyers or doctors or other highly educated people; true? Well the next quote I want you to read slowly.

"He who made us would have been a pitiful bungler, if he had made the rules of our moral conduct a matter of science. For one man of science, there are thousands who are not. What would have become of them? Man was destined for society. His morality, therefore, was to be formed to this object. He was endowed with a sense of right and wrong merely relative to this. This sense is as much a part of his nature, as the sense of hearing, seeing, feeling; it is the true foundation of morality... The moral sense, or conscience, is as much a part of man as his leg or arm. It is given to all human beings in a stronger or weaker degree, as force of members is given them in a greater or less degree. It may be strengthened by exercise, as may any particular limb of the body. This sense is submitted indeed in some degree to the guidance of reason; but it is a small stock which is required for this: even a less one than what we call Common sense. State a moral case to a

> ploughman and a professor. The former will decide it as well, and often better than the latter, because he has not been led astray by artificial rules." --Thomas Jefferson to Peter Carr, 1787. ME 6:257, Papers 12:15

Morality and common sense is what seems to be lacking in most of our legislators. Seeing as how we no longer have common people in office as senators and congressmen this would explain a lot of our troubles. Most are lawyers or doctors or were born into wealthy families and don't have a clue as to normal everyday living. They want all their little programs and laws that do nothing to really make life better for most people. Right about now you may be thinking that I am crazy and need an I love me jacket and a padded room. But calm down and take a real hard look at what we have in office and what they are doing with our lives with the laws they are passing and the programs they are implementing. Now I want you to read this quote again, hopefully it will mean more this time.

> "Unless the mass retains sufficient control over those entrusted with the powers of their government, these will be perverted to their own oppression, and to the perpetuation of wealth and power in the individuals and their families selected for

the trust." --Thomas Jefferson to M. van der Kemp, 1812. ME 13:136

Does it mean more this time and can you see the relevance?

Let me point out some things that will make more sense to you hopefully. Most of the people in office have given up jobs paying a lot more than the salaries they get as senators and members of congress. Why? Power, power over the lives of people. The roles have been completely reversed. What part of public servant don't they and the American people not understand? Not the public serving them and jumping to their tune but they doing as the people say to do.

"[An] act of the Congress of the United States... which assumes powers... not delegated by the Constitution, is not law, but is altogether void and of no force." --Thomas Jefferson: Draft Kentucky Resolutions, 1798. ME 17:383

"An elective despotism was not the government we fought for, but one which should not only be founded on true free principles, but in which the powers of government should be so divided and balanced among general bodies of

magistracy, as that no one could transcend their legal limits without being effectually checked and restrained by the others."
--Thomas Jefferson: Notes on Virginia Q.XIII, 1782. ME 2:163

"When all government, domestic and foreign, in little as in great things, shall be drawn to Washington as the center of all power, it will render powerless the checks provided of one government on another and will become as venal and oppressive as the government from which we separated."
--Thomas Jefferson to Charles Hammond, 1821. ME 15:332

I want you the reader to reread the above quotes slowly. Would you dare say that the people we have in Washington fit the description of the type of corrupt government mentioned above? I wish this were true today that the American people would find it in themselves to stand up and make these people in Washington act, as they should. Stand up for your rights and stick to it, is what Thomas Jefferson would say today. You say, how can you say that, here's how?

> "We will breast... every misfortune save that only of living under a government of unlimited powers. We owe every other sacrifice to ourselves, to our federal brethren, and to the world at large to pursue with temper and perseverance the great experiment which shall prove that man is capable of living in society, governing itself by laws self-imposed, and securing to its members the enjoyment of life, liberty, property and peace; and further to show that even when the government of its choice shall manifest a tendency to degeneracy, we are not at once to despair, but that the will and the watchfulness of its sounder parts will reform its aberrations, recall it to original and legitimate principles, and restrain it within the rightful limits of self-government." --Thomas Jefferson: Declaration and Protest of Virginia, 1825. ME 17:445

> "A free people [claim] their rights as derived from the laws of nature, and not as the gift of their chief magistrate." --Thomas

Jefferson: Rights of British America, 1774. ME 1:209, Papers 1:134

"If this avenue [i.e., the expression of the voice of the whole people] be shut to the call of sufferance, it will make itself heard through that of force, and we shall go on as other nations are doing in the endless circle of oppression, rebellion, reformation; and oppression, rebellion, reformation again; and so on forever." --Thomas Jefferson to Samuel Kercheval, 1816. ME 15:43

These quotes show you how one of the principle Founding Fathers looked at how the government he helped establish was to work and what the people were to do when it didn't' work the way it should. The senators, members of congress and the president work for the American people. They are to do as the nation says to do.

In this chapter I have shown you straight from the Constitution what our legislators jobs and limits are according to the Constitution of the United States. It is up to you to judge if it is being done right. Now I am about to show you some suggested means and ways to fix our elected officials attitudes and job performances. As I have already mentioned there has been a lot of research and talking with many other people to write this book. Below are some of their ideas on how to straighten our public servants out.

1. Don't vote for the party, vote for the individual.

2. Set their pay as the median salary of all the states averaged together.

3. Make them punch a clock and pay them only for time worked.

4. If they are found taking a bribe and found guilty, hang them.

5. If they are trying to pass laws that go against the Constitution, impeach them.

6. Trim all the perks they have, they tell the citizen to tighten their belts so they should lead by example.

7. Demand the removal of the United States from the U.N. and Nafta and

Gatt and any other treaties that give away the sovereignty of the U.S.

8. Put time limits on their stay in the Senate and Congress.

9. Vigorously remind them that they work for the people.

10. Outlaw lobbyist and influence peddling, no more special interests groups.

11. Go back to doing things as the Constitution of The United States dictates.

12. And finally remind them that people remember the Tea Party and all that it entailed.

13. Make sure they and their families are on the same healthcare system we are to use.

Now before you write me off as some sort of domestic terrorist or nut job let me one more time remind you the reader that this is a compiled work. I have talked to broad cross sections of people to write this book. I have talked to young and old, rich and poor, conspiracy theorist, ignorant, and the well educated. The general consensus is that the people in Washington are out of control, our country is being sold, we are broke, our sovereignty is being given away, and the idiots in power don't care.

Now I personally agree with a lot of what has been written in this book, not all but most. I have done my very best to be fair and honest. Some of my favorite quotes are these.

"I have been blamed for saying that a prevalence of the doctrines of consolidation would one day call for reformation or revolution. I answer by asking if a single State of the union would have agreed to the Constitution had it given all powers to the General Government? If the whole opposition to it did not proceed from the jealousy and fear of every State of being subjected to the other States in matters merely its own? And if there is any reason to believe the States more disposed now than then to acquiesce in this general surrender of all their rights and powers to a consolidated government, one and undivided?" --Thomas Jefferson to William Johnson, 1823. ME 15:444

"I may err in my measures, but never shall deflect from the intention to fortify the public liberty by every possible means, and to put it out of the power of the few to riot on the labors of the many." --Thomas Jefferson to John Tyler, 1804. ME 11:33

"[Oppose] with manly firmness [any] invasions on the rights of the people." --Thomas Jefferson: Draft Virginia Constitution, 1776. (*) Papers 1:338

In my understanding this has not been done. The people in Washington are doing everything they can to take total control of our lives. Everything from how to feed and raise our kids to our own medical care. What right do these pompous and arrogant people have to dictate such, no right. What happened to the Constitution?

Let me ask you and the Senate and the Congress and even the President a few simple questions and let's see if we agree.

1. Where does milk come from?
2. What happens if you don't feed the cow?
3. Where does the milk come from?

Now as you have noticed # 1 and # 3 are the same questions but lets look at #2. Milk comes from the cow, that's the easy one. If you don't feed the cow, what happens, it dies of course. That one is easy too, but then answer # 3. Where does the milk come from then? Answer, no more milk.

Now to put it bluntly, this country has been the milk cow to the world ever since WW2.In WW2 we bailed out most of the world and saved their collective butts from the Germans and the Japanese. We have given money to almost all nations, most in the form of loans that they have never repaid. We have given food and technology, and stuck our noses into other countries business for years. Now we are in very bad shape here because of it and we are wondering what to do. A lot of it can be solved with a little common sense. Senators, congressmen, Mr. President, quit worrying about how good your Harvard or whatever school your education come from is and use some common sense for a while in governing. Realize that the cow is dying and something needs to change. The definition of insanity is to do the same thing over and over expecting a different result. But the American people are to be diagnosed with insanity also for not doing something to change things from the way they are back to what we had.

Well let's move on to the next chapter if you are still reading.

Chapter Four
Illegal Aliens and Criminals

This is a very touchy subject with a lot of people. I want to start this with a very blunt and self-explanatory set of quotes.

"Every society has a right to fix the fundamental principles of its association, and to say to all individuals, that if they contemplate pursuits beyond the limits of these principles and involving dangers which the society chooses to avoid, they must go somewhere else for their exercise; that we want no citizens, and still less ephemeral and pseudo-citizens, on such terms. We may exclude them from our territory, as we do persons infected with

> disease." --Thomas Jefferson to William H. Crawford, 1816. ME 15:28

> "Society [has] a right to erase from the roll of its members any one who rendered his own existence inconsistent with theirs; to withdraw from him the protection of their laws, and to remove him from among them by exile, or even by death if necessary."-- Thomas Jefferson to L. H. Girardin, 1815. ME 14:277

Illegal aliens; notice the word illegal! This is so easy to fix. I have been to Mexico and the Philippines and they don't tolerate it in their countries at all. When I went to the Philippines you were told that you could spend 21 days, anything after that you had to have approval from the government. Mexico is a little different but the principle is the same. Japan was a little stricter than that. So what I don't understand is why we in the U.S.A. are having such a problem with this issue and why are we taking flak from the Mexican government over the issue. Find them, arrest them, deport them, and the problem is solved. What is so hard about that? Put up a fence, put up signs in Spanish that say turn around, go back. Why are we not doing like they do in other countries and put them out. In other countries you are shot if you don't turn back. Very simple wouldn't you say?

Yes it sounds harsh, but if you are coming here, come legal and play by the rules. Quit giving them food stamps, Medicare and Medicaid, quit printing everything in Spanish and English. These are simple things that can be done that will stop a lot of the stupidity that is going on right now and it will lower our national debt. What part of illegal does our government not understand? Taxes can be lowered and jobs saved by this very simple solution. I have no animosity towards any person wanting to come to this country, but if you come do it the right way.

Come in legally, learn English, and help make the country better, don't try to make it like the one you left. I would say get a job but I know that's almost impossible here now. Also get rid of the titles African-American, Latino American, Asian-American, if you are American then you are American, no prefixes. In case you are thinking that I am some crazy radical would you back up and slowly reread the part you just read. No other country has those kind of prefixes to their nationality, no other country gives everything to illegals by taking from it's own people.

You now have a president who has stated they want to take money from citizens and give it to illegal aliens to help them live better here illegally. Congress and the senate seem to be ok with this, tell me do you see the problem? Some of these sounds harsh I know but what else can we do. Our jobs are going overseas, Medicare and Medicaid are going broke, everything including road signs is being printed in other languages and no one seems to care. Our government is demanding we learn Spanish in school so our children can function better here because Spanish is so prevalent instead of saying to people coming here to live to learn English.

Someone tell me what is wrong with that picture. Are you not tired of having the global this and the global that rammed down your throat by our government at the cost of your way of life, job, community, freedom, liberty and security?

We have had a lot of turmoil for the last couple of years over illegal aliens and the government has punished people for protecting what's theirs; I know if you watch the news you know what I am talking about. Our leaders in government need to read this and understand it clearly. Also they need to read and understand this next section.

We the People of the United States, in Order to form a more perfect Union, *establish Justice,* insure *domestic Tranquility,* provide for the common *defense,* promote the *general Welfare,* and secure the *Blessings of Liberty* to ourselves and our *Posterity,* do *ordain and establish* this Constitution for the United States of America.

Remember this? This is the preamble to the Constitution of

The United States of America. WE the people of the United States, not Mexico, Haiti, china, or any other country. Is it going to take another revolution to get it through to our government? Like I said, this is the feeling among all classes of people.

What it basically boils down to is this.

1. Send the illegals home.
2. Quit giving them Medicare and Medicaid.
3. No more food stamps.
4. No more jobs for them because they are here illegally.
5. Taxes can be lowered.
6. Crime will go down.
7. More Americans will have jobs and can get off the public dole.

What part of everyday common sense does Washington not get?

Now lets deal with criminals having more rights than law-abiding citizens. If someone is trying to rape my daughter and I shoot him and don't kill him he can sue me. Tell me what is wrong with this picture? If I kill him his family can sue me for a wrongful death. It's crazy don't you think?

It's funny that   you get more time for tax evasion than for murder. There is no punishment for crime anymore.

Meth is a big thing where I'm from. I know of people being busted for the third time and walking the street the next day. Prisons are over crowded all the time. Easy to fix, murderers, rapists, child molesters, and habitual criminals should be taken to the courthouse square and hanged by the neck until dead.

The rope is biodegradable, reusable and environmentally friendly. Appeals; you should get 3. If you are not found innocent by the third time in 3 months then you are hung. How cruel you say, not cruel, cruel is rape, murder, child molestation. Quit worrying about the criminal and focus on the innocent one who had these things happen to them.

Drunk drivers, pot smokers and other crimes of this nature should get punished too. First offence, restore what was stolen or tore up with community service; second offence 2 years hard labor, 3 offences and you hang by the neck until dead. This also applies to thieves who are on their third offence. For crying out loud quit babying these people and putting them in an air conditioned prison with cable and satellite and three squares and a bed.

Quit allowing them to get a college education on your tax

dollars and mine. Put some fear into crime and clean out death row and watch it change. It costs over $40,000 a year per person to keep people on death row. Why are we keeping them there for years and years after they have gotten the death sentence?

 Ok let's go on if you haven't thrown the book away. Gun ownership, everyone over 21 who has a clean record should have one. It would stop a lot of the nonsense going on today. Crime would go down, prisons wouldn't be as crowded, and people would be safer. That's like our schools today having a zero tolerance on fighting. Your child who merely defended itself gets the same punishment as the one who started the fight. Our children are being taught not to defend themselves for fear of being punished, that's crazy don't you think? Simple solutions mentioned above would curtail crime, lower taxes; and make our country safer.

I don't understand how we as a people continue to let the senate and the congress pass laws that give the criminals more rights and more protection than the victims. Why are we letting them deprive us of our ability to protect ourselves? I know that some of the things I've said are drastic and seem cruel to others. But are they really? Are you content to set back and let things go on and get worse? I hear the republicans say this and the democrats that and then the radio talk show hosts go on about them both and nobody has any answers. What happened to common sense? Illegal aliens are illegal, murderers kill people, rape is rape, child molesters molest, and they get a slap on the wrist and are turned loose for the most part. Why is this so? Most are found to commit the crimes again and again. Where is the justice? Why are we as a nation condoning this? So ask yourself this question, am I ok with the criminal having more rights than myself.

Gun control is something the government is big on today. I believe in gun control too; everyone should have one and know how to control it. Mr. Jefferson felt the same way, look at these quotes.

"The constitutions of most of our States assert that all power is inherent in the people; that they may exercise it by themselves in all cases to which they think themselves competent (as in electing their functionaries executive and legislative, and deciding by a jury of themselves in all judiciary cases in which any fact is involved), or they may act by representatives, freely and equally chosen; <u>that it is their right and duty to be at all times armed; that they are entitled to freedom of person, freedom of religion, freedom of property, and freedom of the press.</u>" --Thomas Jefferson to John Cartwright, 1824. ME 16:45

"One loves to possess arms, though they hope never to have occasion for them." --Thomas Jefferson to George Washington, 1796. ME 9:341

"No freeman shall be debarred the use of arms (within his own lands or tenements)." --Thomas Jefferson: Draft Virginia Constitution (with his note added), 1776. Papers 1:353

"The Greeks and Romans had no standing armies, yet they defended themselves. The Greeks by their laws, and the Romans by the spirit of their people, took care to put into the hands of their rulers no such engine of oppression as a standing army. Their system was to make every man

47

a soldier and oblige him to repair to the standard of his country whenever that was reared. This made them invincible; and the same remedy will make us so." --Thomas Jefferson to Thomas Cooper, 1814. ME 14:184

The last quote above is why Switzerland was not taken by the German army, Hitler's advisor told him they could take the country but at a very great expense. By now you are wondering why all this was put in this chapter, here's why.

"Laws are made for men of ordinary understanding and should, therefore, be construed by the ordinary rules of common sense. Their meaning is not to be sought for in metaphysical subtleties which may make anything mean everything or nothing at pleasure." --Thomas Jefferson to William Johnson, 1823. ME 15:450

Amendment 2 - Right to Bear Arms. Ratified 12/15/1791.

A well regulated Militia, being necessary to the security

of a free State, the right of the people to keep and bear Arms, shall not be infringed.

If the laws are made to be understood then the above-mentioned amendment is so simply worded that none can misunderstand it. The amendment is there so when the government gets out of hand the people can do this.

> "We hold these truths to be self-evident, that all men are created equal; that they are endowed by their Creator with inherent and inalienable rights; that among these, are life, liberty, and the pursuit of happiness; that to secure these rights, governments are instituted among men, deriving their just powers from the consent of the governed; that whenever any form of government becomes destructive of these ends, it is the right of the people to alter or abolish it, and to institute new government, laying its foundation on such principles, and organizing its powers in such form, as to them shall seem most likely to effect their safety and happiness." --Declaration of Independence as originally written by

Thomas Jefferson, 1776. ME 1:29, Papers 1:315

"What country can preserve its liberties if its rulers are not warned from time to time that their people preserve the spirit of resistance? Let them take arms. The remedy is to set them right as to facts, pardon and pacify them." --Thomas Jefferson to William Stephens Smith, 1787. ME 6:373, Papers 12:356

"What signify a few lives lost in a century or two? The tree of liberty must be refreshed from time to time with the blood of patriots and tyrants. It is its natural manure." --Thomas Jefferson to William Stephens Smith, 1787. ME 6:373, Papers 12:356

Pretty self-explanatory don't you think? What so many people seem to forget is this, these men, not just Thomas Jefferson, but the men who wrote the Constitution, Bill of Rights and formed our government despised, hated, and loathed one thing. Tyranny! The greatest form of crime there is to mankind as a whole. Now what we have happening in this country is a group of supposed public servants forgetting they work for us, dictating what we can and cannot do. Tyranny in it simplest form, political criminals forcing upon a people a rule by force. From the president on down to the Pelosi woman and most of the senators and members of congress there is no doubt; Tyranny in it's purest form. Let me show you something that they all agreed to, not just Jefferson's idea, but also all the Founding Fathers.

He has combined with others to subject us to a jurisdiction foreign to our constitution, and unacknowledged by our laws; giving his Assent to their Acts of pretended legislation: For imposing taxes on us without our Consent:

For depriving us, in many cases, of the benefits of Trial by Jury:

For taking away our Charters, abolishing our most valuable Laws, and altering fundamentally the Forms of our Governments:

He has made judges dependent on his Will alone, for the tenure of their offices, and the amount and payment of their salaries.

He has erected a multitude of New Offices, and sent hither swarms of Officers to harass our People, and eat out their substance.

He has called together legislative bodies at places unusual, uncomfortable, and distant from the depository of their Public Records, for the sole purpose of fatiguing them into compliance with his measures.

Take a look at the list above and ask yourself the following. Is any of it relevant today? If you say yes then hold on; if you say no let me point out some things. Looking at the list above let's deal with the first on the list.

He has combined with others to subject us to a jurisdiction foreign to our constitution, and unacknowledged by our laws; giving his Assent to their Acts of pretended legislation:

Do you not think that selling this country to China in selling our bonds and debt to them to the point that they can begin to dictate terms is similar? Letting the U.N. send us here and there seems to fit the bill also. When we as American citizens need to worry about what the world court says about what we do; we have a problem.

For imposing taxes on us without our Consent:

Hell, this one is so blatantly obvious it should need no explanation. Look around you at all the crazy taxes we have and I'm sure no one wanted them.

For depriving us, in many cases, of the benefits of Trial by Jury:

Thanks to some unconstitutional laws that they in government have passed we now see this happening on a continual basis. Watch the news and read the papers and you will see it all the time. Ask the families of the Border Patrol agents who are in jail for doing their jobs even though it was politically incorrect.

For taking away our Charters, abolishing our most valuable Laws, and altering fundamentally the Forms of our Governments:

Have you noticed how the Constitution of the United States of America has no meaning? How the senators, members of congress, and what is supposed to be a president doesn't uphold the oaths they swore or affirmed to protect and defend said Constitution. How the Bill of Rights is ignored on a regular basis? Let me show you this.

Article VI - Debts, Supremacy, Oaths

This Constitution, and the Laws of the United States which shall be made in Pursuance thereof; and all Treaties made, or which shall be made, under the Authority of the United States, <u>shall be the supreme Law of the Land; and the Judges in every State shall be bound thereby, any Thing in the Constitution or Laws of any State to the Contrary notwithstanding.</u>

The Senators and Representatives before mentioned, and the Members of the several State Legislatures, and all executive and judicial Officers, both of the United States and of the several States, <u>shall be bound by Oath or Affirmation, to support this Constitution;</u> but no religious Test shall ever be required as a Qualification to any Office or public Trust under the United States.

Notice the above underlined. The Constitution is the supreme law in the land. The people in congress and the senate and the president are bound by oath to support the Constitution and abide by it in their work.

Article II - The Executive Branch

Section 1 - The President

Before he enter on the Execution of his Office, he shall take the following Oath or Affirmation:

"I do solemnly swear (or affirm) that I will faithfully execute the Office of President of the United States, and will to the best of my Ability, preserve, protect and defend the Constitution of the United States."

> Is he doing that or is he doing his best to trample the Constitution and the Bill of Rights in the ground? I would ask the same about our senators and members of Congress?

He has made judges dependent on his Will alone, for the tenure of their offices, and the amount and payment of their salaries.

> What about the man we have as president trying to buy votes for this health care bill by offering judgeships for votes. It has been all over the news.

He has erected a multitude of New Offices, and sent hither swarms of Officers to harass our People, and eat out their substance.

What about all these new agencies and czars we now are getting in Washington and the new taxes being proposed to fund them?

He has called together legislative bodies at places unusual, uncomfortable, and distant from the depository of their Public Records, for the sole purpose of fatiguing them into compliance with his measures.

What do you call all the little summits and private meetings they have had trying to get the votes for a health care reform no one wants? Bribes of billions of dollars to senators home states to get the senator to vote the way he wants. It is all public record and can be checked on at any time.

This chapter is on illegal aliens and criminals. I have outlined to you what are probably the most corrupt and heinous crimes in this country. The selling of your children and grandchildren's birthrights by putting them into indentured servitude before they are born in some cases. The giving away of our country and sovereignty and the citizens of this country being treated as slaves and property that owes all to the people in government. The trampling of our God given rights guaranteed by the Bill of Rights. Oh I know I just insulted someone or hurt his or her little feelings when I mentioned God. I have heard how there is nothing of God in the Declaration of Independence or the Constitution; well look at these quotes and sections.

Article VII - Ratification

The Ratification of the Conventions of nine States, shall be sufficient for the Establishment of this Constitution between the States so ratifying the Same.

Done in Convention by the Unanimous Consent of the States present the Seventeenth Day of September <u>in the Year of our Lord one thousand seven hundred and Eighty seven</u> and of the Independence of the United States of America the Twelfth. In Witness whereof We have hereunto subscribed our Names.

When in the Course of human events, it becomes necessary for one people to dissolve the political bands which have connected them with another, and to assume, among the Powers of the earth, the separate and equal station to which the Laws of Nature <u>and of Nature's God entitle them,</u> a decent respect *to the opinions of mankind requires that they should declare the causes which impel them to the separation.*

We hold these truths to be self-evident, that all men are created equal, that they are endowed <u>by their Creator with certain unalienable Rights</u>, that among these are Life, Liberty, and the pursuit of Happiness. Declaration of Independence 1776

> "Can the liberties of a nation be thought secure when we have removed their only firm basis, a conviction in the minds of the people that these liberties are of the gift of God? That they are not to be violated but with His wrath?" --Thomas Jefferson: Notes on Virginia Q.XVIII, 1782. ME 2:227

> When they wrote these documents and formed the country most of the men were Christian, so get over it. Quit trying to rewrite history to suit yourselves.

Well on to the next chapter

Chapter Five
Impeachment of Elected Officials

Several senators and people in congress told us during (town hall) meetings that they in office didn't answer to us the citizen. Oh yes they do, and they can be fired without voting them out of office. This is straight out of the Constitution of the United States.

Article VI - Debts, Supremacy, Oaths

All Debts contracted and Engagements entered into, before the Adoption of this Constitution, shall be as valid against the United States under this Constitution, as under the Confederation.

This Constitution, and the Laws of the United States which shall be made in Pursuance thereof; and all Treaties made, or which shall be made, under the Authority of the United States, shall be the supreme Law of the Land; and the Judges in every State shall be bound thereby, any Thing in the Constitution or Laws of any State to the Contrary notwithstanding.

The Senators and Representatives before mentioned, and the Members of the several State Legislatures, and all executive and judicial Officers, both of the United States and of the several States, shall be bound by Oath or Affirmation, to support this Constitution; but no religious Test shall ever be required as a Qualification to any Office or public Trust under the United States.

Article II - The Executive Branch

Section 1 - The President

Before he enter on the Execution of his Office, he shall take the following Oath or Affirmation:

"I do solemnly swear (or affirm) that I will faithfully execute the Office of President of the United States, and will to the best of my Ability, preserve, protect and defend the Constitution of the United States."

Notice the above underlined. The Constitution is the supreme law in the land. The people in congress and the senate and the president are bound by oath to support the Constitution and abide by it in their work.

Article II - The Executive Branch Section 4 - Disqualification

The President, Vice President and all civil Officers of the United States, shall be removed from Office on <u>Impeachment</u> for, and Conviction of, <u>Treason</u>, Bribery, or other high Crimes and Misdemeanors.

Now I ask you the reader have you not been shown in the previous chapters how out of control according to the Constitution our people in the senate and congress are. Even the man we have in office as president is bound by oath. You swear or affirm to tell the truth and nothing but the truth when you are on the stand as a witness, you took an oath. These people took an oath to protect and defend the Constitution, which means you uplift it, stay within its borders and enforce the same. Question, are they doing that? If you have ever had to testify in court you know you swear or affirm to tell the truth and nothing but the truth, yes? What happens if you lie and are caught lying? I do believe it is called perjury and is punishable by jail time.

> "[The people] are in truth the only legitimate proprietors of the soil and government."
> --Thomas Jefferson to Pierre Samuel Dupont de Nemours, 1813. ME 19:197

"[It is] the people, to whom all authority belongs."
--Thomas Jefferson to Spencer Roane, 1821. ME 15:328

"We think experience has proved it safer for the mass of individuals composing the society to reserve to themselves personally the exercise of all rightful powers to which they are competent and to delegate those to which they are not competent to deputies named and removable for unfaithful conduct by themselves immediately." --Thomas Jefferson to Pierre Samuel Dupont de Nemours, 1816. ME 14:487

Do you see the difference in the form of government we had then versus what we have now? The Constitution has not changed, being formed, as a republic has not changed, the Bill of Rights has not changed; then what has happened you might ask?

"If once [the people] become inattentive to the public affairs, you and I, and Congress and Assemblies, Judges and Governors, shall all become wolves. It seems to be the law of our general nature, in spite of individual exceptions." --Thomas Jefferson to Edward Carrington, 1787. ME 6:58

"A departure from principle in one instance becomes a precedent for a second; that second for a third; and so on, till the bulk of the society is reduced to be mere automatons of misery, to have no sensibilities left but for sin and suffering." --Thomas Jefferson to Samuel Kercheval, 1816. ME 15:40

"Our legislators are not sufficiently apprised of the rightful limits of their power: that their true office is to declare and enforce only our natural rights and duties and to take none of them from us. No man has a natural right to commit aggression on the equal rights of another, and this is all from which the laws ought to restrain him; every man is under the natural duty of contributing to the necessities of the society, and this is all the laws should enforce on him; and, no man having a natural right to be the judge between himself and another, it is his natural duty to submit to the umpirage of an impartial third. When the laws have declared and enforced all this, they have fulfilled their functions; and the idea is quite unfounded that on entering into society we give up any natural right. The trial of every law by one of these texts would lessen much the labors of our legislators and lighten equally our municipal codes." --Thomas Jefferson to Francis Gilmer, 1816. ME 15:24

"Congress have no... natural or necessary powers, nor any powers but such as are given them by the Constitution." --Thomas Jefferson: Parliamentary Manual, 1800. ME 2:342

"Withdrawn such a distance from the eye of their constituents, and these so dispersed as to be inaccessible to public information, and particularly to that of the conduct of their own representatives, they will form the most corrupt government on earth if the means of their corruption be not prevented." --Thomas Jefferson to George Washington, 1792. ME 8:345

These all are there to show you how far this country has fallen from what it was intended to be. Most people are under the impression that nothing can be done. People can get together and change our circumstances in this country. Remember that you can vote them out and can demand that the senate impeach. Remember that the people in congress and the senate work for you not you for them. Quit whining about the way it is and look at who you vote for.

We need men and women of good character in office who are reminded that they work for the people and can easily be removed. Term limits can be enforced without being made law; vote them out. There has been a war going on in this country for years that most people don't see. The long-term people in office have been at war with the people of this country. Freedom, liberty, prosperity, people's rights have all been attacked and slowly been taken away. Notice that you have the same old people in Washington just a different brand name at different times. Here is a list of what people I have talked to says is wrong in the country

1. You have had the same bunch of crooks there for years.

2. They are only lining their own pockets. Why would someone give up a job making millions to get paid a little over $110,000 a year?

3. They in government are giving our country away, most of it to China.

4. We need to repeal a lot of stupid laws that only benefit a few.

5. We need to go back to the gold and silver standard and get rid of the Federal Reserve.

6. Term limits are needed.

7. The democratic and republican parties are corrupt and need to be cleaned out.

8. Money is too much of the election process due to the above-mentioned parties.

9. Due to the mentioned above no common and poor person can run for office.

10. Get the U.S. out of the United Nations, the GATT and NAFTA treaties and stop importing so much and make it here instead.

11. Get the government out of our lives as much as possible.

12. Criminals have more rights than their victims.

13. Get rid of the IRS and lower taxes. The fair tax would be one that taxes by buying stuff because then

even people here illegally would have to pay it.

14. Most people believe that the people in Washington are out of touch and out of control.

15. We don't need or want socialism or communism in this country.

16. Insurance companies have too much power and control over things.

17. We need to return to the Constitutional way of running this country.

18. Quit giving our sovereignty away with treaties that bind this country from prospering and elevates other countries.

19. Put America first in America.

20. We have a bill of rights, leave it alone and abide by it.

These are but a few of many things that people are saying are wrong or need to be done in our country. We the people have the ability to stop the insanity and reclaim the country. The United States can once again be what it was, a country of freedom, liberty, prosperity and honor.

Article I - The Legislative Branch   Section 3 - The Senate

The Senate shall have the sole Power to try all Impeachments. When sitting for that Purpose, they shall be on Oath or Affirmation. When the President of the United States is tried, the Chief Justice shall preside: And no Person shall be convicted without the Concurrence of two thirds of the Members present.

Judgment in Cases of Impeachment shall not extend further than to removal from Office, and disqualification to hold and enjoy any Office of honor, Trust or Profit under the United States: but the Party convicted shall nevertheless be liable and subject to Indictment, Trial, Judgment and Punishment, according to Law.

The power to change this country is in the hands of the people. Elect men and women on the merits of their character not their party affiliation. If the people get together and stand together and demand their rights that the people that they have elected abide by the Constitution of the United States this country cannot fail. Our republic was at one time the greatest nation, country, civilization that has ever been on earth. Everyone wanted to come here. I am a student of history and this maxim is true, " Those who forget the past are doomed to repeat it."

Here are the steps " *We The People* "need to take.

1. Get organized.　　Get a working plan on what needs to be done and corrected. Do this with seriousness and prayer, here's why.

"The God who gave us life gave us liberty at the same time; the hand of force may destroy, but cannot disjoin them." --Thomas Jefferson: Rights of British America, 1774. ME 1:211, Papers 1:135

"I sincerely pray that all the members of the human family may, in the time prescribed by the Father of us all, find themselves securely established in the enjoyment of life, liberty, and happiness." --Thomas Jefferson: Reply to Ellicot Thomas, et al., 1807. ME 16:290

"[These are] the rights which God and the laws have given equally and independently to all." --Thomas Jefferson: Rights of British America, 1774. ME 1:185, Papers 1:121

"How necessary was the care of the Creator in making

the moral principle so much a part of our constitution as that no errors of reasoning or of speculation might lead us astray from its observance in practice." --Thomas Jefferson to Thomas Law, 1814. ME 14:139

2. Petition, petition, and then petition some more.

But when a long train of abuses and usurpations, pursuing invariably the same Object evinces a design to reduce them under absolute Despotism, it is their right, it is their duty, to throw off such Government, and to provide new Guards for their future security. --Such has been the patient sufferance of these Colonies; and such is now the necessity which constrains them to alter their former Systems of Government. Declaration of Independence 1776.

"Were [a right] to be refused, or to be so shackled by regulations, not necessary for... peace and safety... as to render its use impracticable,.... it would then be an injury, of which we should be entitled to demand redress." --Thomas Jefferson: Report on Navigation of the Mississippi, 1792. ME 3:178

Now I know some of these quotes are being repeated but with good reason. Over the years with little pushes and a little changing of history people have forgotten the power they were given in this country.

3. Demand impeachments of those Senators, members of Congress and even the President who are guilty of going against the Constitution.

Article II - The Executive Branch

Section 1 - The President

Before he enter on the Execution of his Office, he shall take the following Oath or Affirmation:

"I do solemnly swear (or affirm) that I will faithfully execute the Office of President of the United States, and will to the best of my Ability, preserve, protect and defend the Constitution of the United States."

Section 4 - Disqualification

The President, Vice President and all civil Officers of the United States, shall be removed from Office on Impeachment for, and Conviction of, Treason, Bribery, or other high Crimes and Misdemeanors.

It my understanding that perjury is a felony or a high misdemeanor.

Article VI - Debts, Supremacy, Oaths

This Constitution, and the Laws of the United States which shall be made in Pursuance thereof; and all Treaties made, or which shall be made, under the Authority of the United States, shall be the supreme Law of the Land; and the Judges in every State shall be bound thereby, any Thing in the Constitution or Laws of any State to the Contrary notwithstanding.

The Senators and Representatives before mentioned, and the Members of the several State Legislatures, and all executive and judicial Officers, both of the United States and of the several States, shall be bound by Oath or Affirmation, to support this Constitution; but no religious Test shall ever be required as a Qualification to any Office or public Trust under the United States.

Article III - The Judicial Branch

Section 3 - Treason

Treason against the United States, shall consist only in levying War against them, or in adhering to their Enemies, giving them Aid and Comfort. No Person shall be convicted of Treason unless on the Testimony of two Witnesses to the same overt Act, or on Confession in open Court.

I can say number three because of this.

We the People of the United States, in Order to form a more perfect Union, establish Justice, insure domestic Tranquility, provide for the common defence, promote the general Welfare, and secure the Blessings of Liberty to ourselves and our Posterity, do ordain and establish this Constitution for the United States of America.

"The ultimate arbiter is the people of the

Union." --Thomas Jefferson to William Johnson, 1823. ME 15:451

"In free governments the rulers are the servants and the people their superiors and sovereigns." Benjamin Franklin

"Manfully maintain our good old principle of cherishing and fortifying the rights and authorities of the people in opposition to those who fear them, who wish to take all power from them and to transfer all to Washington." --Thomas Jefferson to Nathaniel Macon, 1826. FE 10:378

You have every right to tell them your grievances and demand they stop what they are doing.

Amendment 1 - Freedom of Religion, Press, Expression. Ratified 12/15/1791.

Congress shall make no law respecting an establishment of religion, or prohibiting the free exercise thereof; or abridging the freedom of speech, or of the press; or the right of the people peaceably to assemble, and to petition the Government for a redress of grievances.

Amendment 10 - Powers of the States and People. Ratified 12/15/1791.

The powers not delegated to the United States by the Constitution, nor prohibited by it to the States, are reserved to the States respectively, or to the people.

> Take the time to look into the laws in this country and see how many of them go against the Constitution and the Bill of Rights.

4. If they won't do #3 then remind them again that they work for us, the citizens of the United States. Remind them of the Tea Party that the people had over 200 years ago. If they still will not listen then The People of the United States have 2 choices.

1. Do nothing and let it continue to ruin your children's and your grandchildren's lives. Let these pompous, arrogant, and preening idiots take all your rights and sell the country.

2. Warn them that we have had enough of the insanity, vote them out, and demand they abide by the Constitution. If they won't do it, have another Tea Party for real

and take back the country. How can I say that? Here's how.

Amendment 1 - Freedom of Religion, Press, Expression. Ratified 12/15/1791.

Congress shall make no law respecting an establishment of religion, or prohibiting the free exercise thereof; or abridging the freedom of speech, or of the press; or the right of the people peaceably to assemble, and to petition the Government for a redress of grievances.

"What country can preserve its liberties if its rulers are not warned from time to time that their people preserve the spirit of resistance? Let them take arms. The remedy is to set them right as to facts, pardon and pacify them." --Thomas Jefferson to William Stephens Smith, 1787. ME 6:373, Papers 12:356

"The spirit of resistance to government is so valuable on certain occasions, that I wish it to be always kept alive. It will often be exercised when wrong, but better so than not to be exercised at all. I like a little rebellion now and then. It is like a storm in the atmosphere." --Thomas Jefferson to Abigail Adams, 1787.

"Most codes extend their definitions of treason to acts not really against one's country. They do not distinguish between acts against the government, and acts against the oppressions of the government. The latter are virtues, yet have furnished more victims to the executioner than the former, because real treasons are rare; oppressions frequent. The unsuccessful strugglers against tyranny have been the chief martyrs of treason laws in all countries." --Thomas Jefferson: Report on Spanish Convention, 1792.

Now I want to say something to you the reader. I hope that you don't think that I am some crazy radical, wannabe domestic terrorist, or some ultra right wing conservative. I am none of the aforementioned list. I am an American citizen who can't find a job, who is tired of the government taking everything I have when I have a job. Who is also tired of having my rights trampled on and cast aside. A simple man who likes to read and study our history, that appreciates the rights and privileges given us in our founding documents. A man that doesn't want his children and grandchildren made indentured servants for some government or God forbid some global government.

When I read about our history in the old history books I grew up with I read of a country that promised life, liberty, the pursuit of happiness. A country that has saved the world from tyranny and oppression more than once. Helped just about every country in the world at one time or another and never really took anything in return. A country that everyone in the world wanted to come to and make a life for themselves. A nation known for its honor, bravery, skill and way of life. This is not what we have now.

We have now an empty shell of a country. A country now known for the crookedness of it's politicians, excesses, wastefulness, and ignorance of it's people. A country of servitude that really doesn't make anything of quality and has become a service based nation. A broken country whose money is worthless and is backed by nothing but paper. A laughing stock that can be threatened and attacked with impunity. Does any of this make sense to you the reader? Do you in any way identify with any of the mentioned above? Are you tired of the same old crap we are getting from our elected officials? Would you like to see a return to greatness in this country where your children and grandchildren live?

If you said yes to and agreed to the things above then get off your butt and start doing something about it. I have shown what I think are ways of going about changing the situation. They can't put everyone in jail; they can't stop everyone. (They) being the people in government who are circumventing the Constitution and the Bill of Rights. I have talked to conspiracy theorist and other groups who are labeled as fringe groups. Some of what they say is true. When you take the time to investigate their claims you find out some of it is true. But then you have the media machine that tells you it is all bull and writes him or her off as crazy. It is this same media machine that the people in government use to run people in the ground and destroy their reputations. There is very little truth in reporting any more, most is told with a very liberal slant. I hate to say it but most reporting and newsgathering is done with a very obvious slant. What happened to objective reporting? What happened to if your in the wrong your in the wrong no matter who or what you are?

Now I'm pretty sure if this book sells well the media that we have today is going to try and make a liar out of me. I am also sure that they are going to paint a pretty bad picture of anyone who agrees with the contents of the book. I don't know about you but I've had it with PC, political correctness as it's known. Look this stuff up in the book and prove it to yourself, don't take my word for it. Due to the people not keeping an eye on the government we now have a group in the halls of power that think they answer to no one. I want you to read this quote and tell your people in Washington and myself what you think.

"When the representative body have lost the confidence of their constituents, when they have notoriously made sale of their most valuable rights, when they have assumed to themselves powers which the people never put into their hands, then, indeed, their continuing in office becomes dangerous to the State, and calls for an

exercise of the power of dissolution."
--Thomas Jefferson: Rights of British
America, 1774. ME 1:204, Papers 1:131

Has this happened and have you had enough of their insanity? I wish to bring to your attention the last quotes that sum up the position the American people are in today. Please read slowly and carefully.

"I am... against all violations of the Constitution to silence by force and not by reason the complaints or criticisms, just or unjust, of our citizens against the conduct of their agents." --Thomas Jefferson to Elbridge Gerry, 1799. ME 10:78

> "The greatest [calamity] which could befall [us would be] submission to a government of unlimited powers." --Thomas Jefferson: Declaration and Protest of Virginia, 1825. ME 17:445

> "Were we directed from Washington when to sow and when to reap, we should soon want bread." --Thomas Jefferson: Autobiography, 1821. ME 1:122

> "We must make our election between

economy and liberty, or profusion and servitude." --Thomas Jefferson to Samuel Kercheval, 1816. ME 15:39

"On every question of construction carry ourselves back to the time when the Constitution was adopted, recollect the spirit manifested in the debates and instead of trying what meaning may be squeezed out of the text or invented against it, conform to the probable one in which it was passed." --Thomas Jefferson to William Johnson, 1823. ME 15:449

The quote that was quoted last is something that our elected officials should go by without question. This would do one of two things where they are concerned. Either excite them to true service or shame them into quitting for the betterment of the country. On the last page you will find a, for a better word, another declaration of independence. I say that because the Declaration of Independence was a letter to a corrupt government that would not listen to the people it controlled. It was a letter to address grievances and wrongs being done to the people in this country before it became the United States of America. How much more serious and spine chilling these next quotes when thought of in this perspective.

When in the Course of human events, it becomes necessary for one people to dissolve the political bands which have connected them with another, and to assume, among the Powers of the earth, the separate and equal station to which the Laws of Nature and of Nature's God entitle them, a decent respect to the opinions of mankind requires that they should declare the causes which impel them to the separation. Declaration of Independence 1776

We hold these truths to be self-evident, that all men are created equal, that they are endowed by their Creator with certain unalienable Rights, that among these are Life, Liberty, and the pursuit of Happiness. That to secure these rights, Governments are instituted among Men, deriving their just powers from the consent of the governed, That whenever any Form of Government becomes destructive of these ends, it is the Right of the People to alter or to abolish it, and to institute new Government, laying its foundation on such principles and organizing its powers in such form, as to them shall seem most likely to effect their Safety and Happiness. Prudence, indeed, will dictate that Governments long established should not be changed for light and transient causes; and accordingly all experience hath shown, that mankind are more disposed to suffer, while evils are sufferable, than to right themselves by abolishing the forms to which they are accustomed. But when a long train of abuses and usurpations, pursuing invariably the same Object evinces a design to reduce them under absolute Despotism, it is their right, it is their duty, to throw off such Government, and to provide new Guards for their future security. --Such has been the patient sufferance of these Colonies; and such is now the necessity which constrains them to alter their former Systems of Government.   Declaration of Independence 1776

He has refused his Assent to Laws, the most wholesome and necessary for the public good.

He has called together legislative bodies at places unusual, uncomfortable, and distant from the depository of their Public Records, for the sole purpose of fatiguing them into compliance with his measures.

He has made judges dependent on his Will alone, for the tenure of their offices, and the amount and payment of their salaries.

He has erected a multitude of New Offices, and sent hither swarms of Officers to harass our People, and eat out their substance.

He has combined with others to subject us to a jurisdiction foreign to our constitution, and unacknowledged by our laws; giving his Assent to their Acts of pretended legislation:

For imposing taxes on us without our Consent:

For depriving us, in many cases, of the benefits of Trial by Jury:

For taking away our Charters, abolishing our most valuable Laws, and altering fundamentally the Forms of our Governments:

In every stage of these Oppressions We have Petitioned for Redress in the most humble terms: Our repeated Petitions have been answered only by repeated injury. A Prince, whose character is thus marked by every act which may define a Tyrant, is unfit to be the ruler of a free People.

We have warned them from time to time of attempts by their legislature to extend an unwarrantable jurisdiction over us. We have reminded them of the circumstances of our emigration and settlement here. We have appealed to their native justice and magnanimity, and we have conjured them by the ties of our common kindred to disavow these usurpations, which would inevitably interrupt our connections and correspondence. They too have been deaf to the voice of justice and of consanguinity. We must, therefore, acquiesce in the necessity, which denounces our Separation, and hold them, as we hold the rest of mankind, Enemies in War, in Peace Friends.

Appealing to the Supreme Judge of the world for the rectitude of our intentions, do, in the Name, and by the Authority of the good People of these Colonies, solemnly publish and declare, That these United Colonies are, and of Right ought to be Free and Independent States

And that as Free and Independent States, they have full Power to levy War, conclude Peace, contract Alliances, establish Commerce, and to do all other Acts and Things which Independent States may of right do. And for the support of this Declaration, with a firm reliance on the Protection of Divine Providence, we mutually pledge to each other our Lives, our Fortunes and our sacred Honor. Declaration of Independence 1776

I would find it amusing that the above sections of the Declaration of Independence fit in today's setting so well if it wasn't so terrifying. I took the time and liberty of taking out sections and putting them in the order they are in, in complete sense making sets so no one can argue. Do they, the quotes above not describe the problems we are having today? Do you not see what our Founding Fathers thought of the abuse and tyranny they were under? Their response is what brought this country into being. Are you satisfied with what we now have in government?

One last set of quotes for you to think on.

> "A first attempt to recover the right of self-government may fail, so may a second,

a third, etc. But as a younger and more instructed race comes on, the sentiment becomes more and more intuitive, and a fourth, a fifth, or some subsequent one of the ever renewed attempts will ultimately succeed... To attain all this, however, rivers of blood must yet flow, and years of desolation pass over; yet the object is worth rivers of blood and years of desolation. For what inheritance so valuable can man leave to his posterity?" --Thomas Jefferson to John Adams, 1823. ME 15:465

"The oppressed should rebel, and they will continue to rebel and raise disturbance until their civil rights are fully restored to them and all partial distinctions, exclusions and incapacitations are removed." --Thomas Jefferson: Notes on Religion, 1776. Papers 1:548

"Rebellion to tyrants is obedience to God." --Thomas Jefferson: his motto.

"Single acts of tyranny may be ascribed to the accidental opinion of a day; but a series of oppressions, begun at a distinguished period and pursued unalterably through every change of ministers, too plainly prove a deliberate, systematic plan of reducing [a people] to slavery." --Thomas Jefferson: Rights of British America, 1774. (*) ME 1:193, Papers 1:125

I want you the reader to take the last page of this book and check what you agree with. If you wish to be like John Hancock sign it really large. Once that is done mail it to your senator or congressman. Or sign it and mail them the book, give them some easy to understand reading materiel that makes a point.

I talked to a guy who wants things to change but he made a good point when I said do something. He said he has been ready to charge the hill but when he looks behind him there's no one with him. Get out there and do something together. They can't put everyone in jail, they can't ruin everyone financially, if you want back what has been lost then we have to show them we are willing to do this.

"Whensoever the General Government assumes undelegated powers, its acts are unauthoritative, void, and of no force." --Thomas Jefferson: Draft Kentucky Resolutions, 1798. ME 17:380

"[An] act of the Congress of the United States... which assumes powers... not delegated by the Constitution, is not law, but is altogether void and of no force." --Thomas Jefferson: Draft Kentucky Resolutions, 1798. ME 17:383

"When patience has begotten false estimates of its motives, when wrongs are pressed because it is believed they will be borne, resistance becomes morality." --Thomas Jefferson to M. deStael, 1807. ME 11:282

"To preserve [the] independence [of the people,] we must not let our rulers load us with perpetual debt. We must make our election between economy and liberty, or profusion and servitude. If we run into such debts as that we must be taxed in our meat and in our drink, in our necessaries and our comforts, in our labors and our amusements, for our callings and our creeds, as the people of England are, our people, like them, must come to labor sixteen hours in the twenty-four, give the earnings of fifteen of these to the government for their debts and daily expenses, and the sixteenth being insufficient to afford us bread, we must live, as they now do, on oatmeal and potatoes, have no time to think, no means of calling the mismanagers to account, but be glad to obtain subsistence by hiring ourselves to rivet their chains on the necks of our fellow-sufferers." --Thomas Jefferson to Samuel Kercheval, 1816. ME 15:39

"[When] corruption.. has prevailed in those offices [of]... government and [has] so familiarized itself as that men otherwise honest could look on it without horror,... [then we must] be alive to the suppression of this odious practice and... bring to punishment and brand with eternal disgrace every man guilty of it, whatever be his station." --Thomas Jefferson to W. C. C. Claiborne, 1804. (*)

"[Montesquieu wrote in Spirit of the Laws, VIII,c.12:] 'When once a republic is corrupted, there is no possibility of remedying any of the growing evils but by removing the corruption and restoring its lost principles; every other correction is either useless or a new evil.'" --Thomas Jefferson: copied into his Commonplace Book.

I have included these last quotes as warning light to the people in this country. Remember that the quotes are from the writer of the Declaration of Independence and a former president of the country he helped form. Do you the reader want the kind of government we have now or the kind we lost? Fill in the lines on the last page with an I agree or an I disagree. If you have the nerve sign it and mail it to your senator or member of congress. If you want to sign it and check what you agree with and mail them the book that's even better, it is written on a 10th grade level so even they could understand.

We the people of the United States with a heavy heart and a serious mind make these statements of grievance.

1. *We want the United States of America withdrawn from the N.A.F.T.A and G.A.T.T. treaties so that we reclaim our manufacturing jobs.*

I agree _____

I disagee _____ .

2. The healthcare reform bill was passed against the will of the people of this country and done so illegally. Repeal it!

I agree _____

I disagee _____.

3. Illegal aliens are to be caught and sent home. No more food stamps, Medicare and Medicaid benefits are to be given to them.

I agree _____

I disagee _____.

Cut here ✂

4. You the people we elected work for us and answer to the people whose tax dollars pay your overpriced way of life. Do as we say or get put out!

I agree _____

I disagee _____.

5. We want all those who voted for the healthcare bill impeached and removed from office. Also Mr. Obama is to be impeached along with them for perjury and violations of oath of office.

I agree _____

I disagee _____.

✂ Cut here

6. China will no longer get most favored nation status and will have tariffs applied to their products.

I agree _____

I disagee _____.

7. You will as senators and members of congress pass the laws necessary to stop giving yourselves automatic pay raises.

I agree _____

I disagee _____.

Cut here

8. Senators and members of congress and future presidents must work within the guidelines given by the Constitution of the United States.

I agree _____

I disagee _____ .

9. Laws that have given our sovereignty away are to be repealed.

I agree _____

I disagee _____ .

✂ Cut here

10. Until the budget is balanced and our national debt is paid there will be no more pay raises for senators and members of congress. Your pay needs to be made the average salary of the population of the United States.

I agree _____

I disagee _____ .

Cut here

11. You as members of congress and the senate will have your perks trimmed, i.e. no more taxpayer money to pay for your cars, trips, parties and such. You have told the American people to tighten their belts so lead by example. Besides you work for us, so we demand the above.

I agree _____

I disagee _____.

12. We want the laws gone through and those that are unconstitutional repealed. Remember this is not a democracy but a republic. You work for the people.

I agree _____

I disagee _____.

13. Quit giving our jobs, money, and sovereignty away, put America and its problems first.

I agree _____

I disagee _____.

✂ Cut here

14. In the spirit of the first Declaration of Independence this is being sent to you senators, congressmen, and president. To put it plainly we the people have had enough of the insanity from Washington. Either go back to working by the guidelines given in the founding documents of this country or prepare for the revolution that comes next. This is the same circumstances that the King of England could have avoided if he had listened to our founding fathers. In the spirit of reconciliation we ask you to do the aforementioned above to save this republic.

I agree _____

I disagee _____.

102